AMAZING SCIENCE

Energy

Heat, Light, and Fuel

Written by Darlene R. Stille
Illustrated by Sheree Boyd

Special thanks to our advisers for their expertise:

Paul Ohmann, Ph.D., Assistant Professor of Physics
University of St. Thomas, St. Paul, Minnesota

Susan Kesselring, M.A., Literacy Educator
Rosemount-Apple Valley-Eagan (Minnesota) School District

PICTURE WINDOW BOOKS
MINNEAPOLIS, MINNESOTA

Managing Editor: Bob Temple
Creative Director: Terri Foley
Editor: Nadia Higgins
Editorial Adviser: Andrea Cascardi
Copy Editor: Laurie Kahn
Designer: John Moldstad
Page production: Picture Window Books
The illustrations in this book were prepared digitally.

Picture Window Books
5115 Excelsior Boulevard
Suite 232
Minneapolis, MN 55416
1-877-845-8392
www.picturewindowbooks.com

Printed in the United States of America.

Library of Congress Cataloging-in-Publication Data
Stille, Darlene R.
Energy : heat, light, and fuel / written by Darlene Stille ;
illustrated by Sheree Boyd.
v. cm. — (Amazing science)
Includes bibliographical references and index.
Contents: Energy gets things done—Where energy comes from—
How energy works for you—Stored and working energy—
Saving energy—Experiments—Fun facts.
ISBN 1-4048-0249-5 (lib. bdg.)
1. Force and energy—Juvenile literature. 2. Power resources—
Juvenile literature. [1. Force and energy. 2. Power resources.]
I. Boyd, Sheree, ill. II. Title. III. Series.
QC73.4 .S75 2004
531'.6—dc22
2003016438

Table of Contents

Energy Gets Things Done

It's morning. You stretch your arms out wide. You jump out of bed. You are full of energy. You use that energy to get things done!

Energy gets lots of things done. There are many forms of energy. Energy heats your house. It lights up lamps. It makes cars, trucks, and buses go.

How Does Energy Work?

Sometimes energy is stored inside things. It's not being used, but it's ready if you need it. Get set to throw a ball. Pull your arm back. Your arm has stored energy.

Swing your arm and let go of the ball.
Your arm puts the stored energy to use.

It's time for breakfast. You eat a bowl
of cereal and drink a glass of orange juice.

The cereal and juice have energy stored inside them. Energy stored inside food is called chemical energy.

FUN FACT

Chemical energy in batteries can be used to make a flashlight beam.
Chemical energy in gasoline can be used to make a car whiz by.

9

Your body breaks up the food. The food releases energy that you use to catch a bus, play basketball, and do everything else throughout your day. Energy of motion is called kinetic energy.

Energy is always changing forms. Your body turns chemical energy from food into kinetic energy.

Rub your hands together very quickly. What happens? Your hands get warm. You used kinetic energy to make heat energy.

Where Does Energy Come From?

Walk through a park on a sunny day. See how bright the flowers look. Feel how hot a park bench gets.

Energy from the sun makes the day bright and hot. Most energy on earth comes from the sun. Energy from the sun is called solar energy.

FUN FACT

Some people put big, shiny panels on the roofs of their houses. These panels turn solar energy into heat energy. People use the heat energy to keep the insides of their houses warm.

14

Water from a river tumbles over a rocky cliff. It makes a beautiful waterfall. There is energy in the falling water.

People build dams in rivers to create waterfalls they can use. The energy in water falling over the dam is used to generate electric energy. Electric energy lights up lamps. It makes your TV, air conditioner, and refrigerator work.

FUN FACT

Energy from wind turns a windmill. In the past, windmills would grind up corn. Today, windmills produce electricity.

You make a campfire by burning wood. Wood is a fuel. Some energy comes from burning fuels.

Coal, crude oil, and natural gas are also fuels. They are called fossil fuels. Fossil fuels come from plants and animals that lived before dinosaurs walked the earth!

Gasoline comes from crude oil. Every time you ride in a car, you are using fossil fuels. Most people use fossil fuels to heat their homes. Many power plants burn fossil fuels to make electricity.

Fossil fuels are being used up quickly. One day they will be gone. People will have to find new ways to make their cars run and to heat their homes.

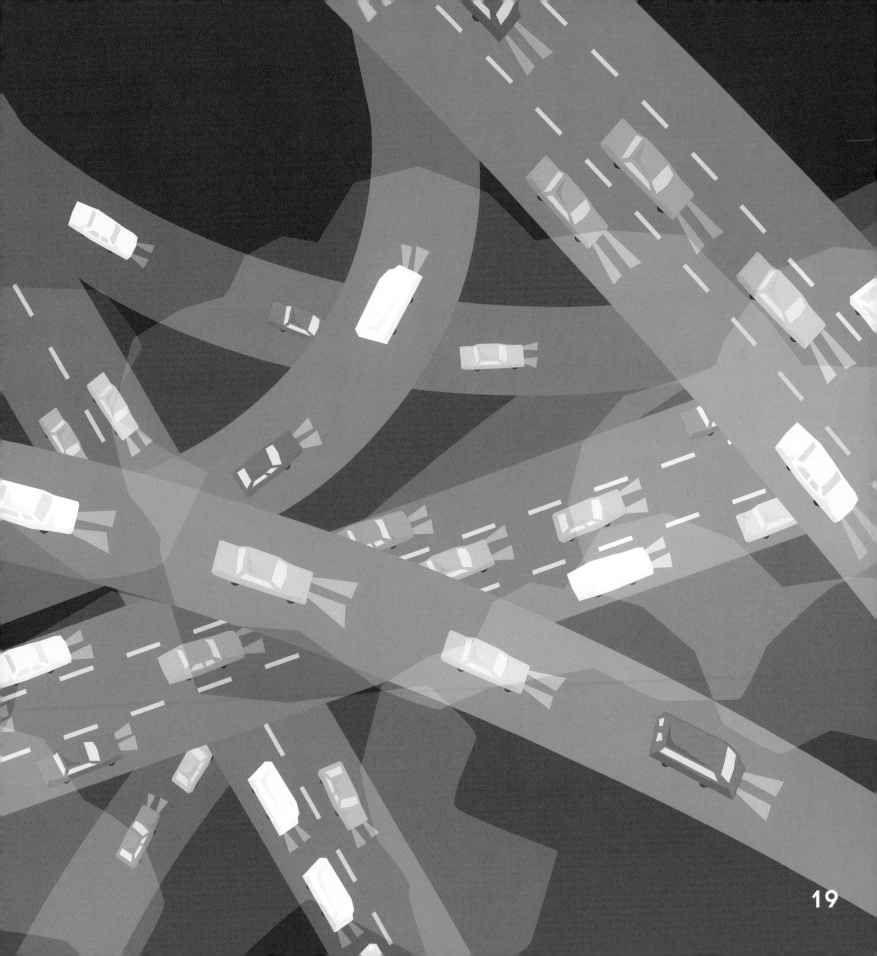

Saving Energy

You can help save fossil fuels. Take the bus instead of a car. Wear a sweater instead of turning up the heat. Turn off the lights when you leave a room.

Doing little things to save energy can make a big difference.

Make a Pinwheel

What you need:
a square sheet of construction paper
scissors
a ruler
a sharpened pencil with an eraser
a pin

What you do:
1. Make sure that your sheet of construction paper is square. If it is rectangular, take one corner and bring it to the opposite edge of the paper. Make a fold. The fold looks like a triangle. Cut off the strip of paper that sticks out above the triangle.
2. Using the ruler and pencil, draw two diagonal lines across the square paper. Draw each line from corner to corner. The lines will cross in the middle of the paper to make an X.
3. Use the tip of the pencil to poke a small hole through the paper where the lines cross.
4. Use the scissors to cut along the lines, but don't cut all the way. Stop cutting about 1 inch (2½ centimeters) from the center. The cuts make four pieces shaped like triangles.
5. Take the left corner of a triangle. Gently fold it in so that the point touches the center of the paper. Be careful not to crease the paper. Do this with the three other triangles. Hold all four points against the center.
6. Get an adult to help you now. Push the pin through the points at the center of the paper. Be careful not to stick yourself with the pin.
7. Lay the pencil down on a table. Push the pin into the eraser. You have made a pinwheel.

Hold up your pinwheel by the pencil. Make some wind by blowing on the pinwheel. What happens? Can you see how wind energy makes the pinwheel spin?

Fuel for Thought

First Fires
People learned to build fires about 1½ million years ago.
Fire gives off heat energy. These early people learned to use
fire to cook their food and to keep them warm.

Hot Rocks
Some energy comes from hot rocks deep inside the earth.
The rocks heat underground water. The water turns into steam.
Pipes bring the steam to a power plant. The steam turns big
machines that make electricity.

Waves of Energy
Energy brings sound and pictures to your TV. Sound and
pictures ride through the air on invisible waves of energy.

Oily Clothes
Petroleum is another name for crude oil. Deep wells bring
petroleum up from the ground. Petroleum gets turned into
many things, such as gasoline and heating oil. It also gets
turned into plastics and cloth. You might be wearing
something made from petroleum.

Loads of Coal
The earth has more coal than any other kind of fossil fuel.
There is still enough coal to last about 200 years.

Glossary

chemical energy–energy stored in food and other substances.
　　　Chemical energy is released when the substances are broken down.
coal–a black or dark brown rock that can burn
crude oil–a thick brown or black liquid that comes from deep inside the earth.
　　　Crude oil is also called petroleum.
dam–dirt, rocks, or cement put across a river to stop the water from going through.
　　　Dams create waterfalls.
fuel–anything that can be burned to give off energy
kinetic energy–the energy of things in motion
natural gas–a gas made in the earth that can be burned
power plant–a place where electricity is made for entire cities or regions

To Learn More

At the Library

Bradley, Kimberly Brubaker. *Energy Makes Things Happen*. New York: HarperCollins, 2003.

Harlow, Rosie and Sally Morgan. *Energy and Power*. New York: Kingfisher, 1995.

Weber, Rebecca. *Feel the Power: Energy All Around*. Minneapolis: Compass Point Books, 2002.

Zemlicka, Shannon. *From Oil to Gas*. Minneapolis: Lerner Publications, 2003.

On the Web

Fact Hound offers a safe, fun way to find Web sites related to this book.
All of the sites on Fact Hound have been researched by our staff.
http://www.facthound.com

1. Visit the Fact Hound home page.
2. Enter a search word related to this book,
   or type in this special code: 1404802495.
3. Click the FETCH IT button.

Your trusty Fact Hound will fetch the best sites for you!

Index